How My
rescue
DOG
rescued
ME

 PUBLISHING

photography by:
{ **julie johnson** }

ON THE COVER

Poor little Kiwi was rescued from horrendously filthy conditions. At 5 ½ months she was listless and undoubtably uncared for. It took two shampoos to rid this darling pup of the stench she was found in.

Kiwi had never been outside or had a breath of fresh air until her rescue family came along.

"She still has some emotional issues, even after eight years of me spoiling her. She still cowers when I pick her up. She sleeps in her princess bed during the day, and at night she sleeps on a pillow next to her human. She is taken care of in a way she truly deserves.

"I can't imagine my life without her!"

meet {*kiwi*}

8 yrs. old
Yorkie/Poodle Mix

How My rescue **DOG** rescued *Me*

Copyright © 2017 Photography by Julie Johnson, Vine Images Inc.
Edited by Lesley Terry

Published by KPT Publishing
Minneapolis, Minnesota 55406
www.KPTPublishing.com

ISBN 978-1-944833-00-8

Design and production by Koechel Peterson and Associates, Minneapolis, Minnesota

First printing March 2017

10 9 8 7 6 5 4 3 2 1

Printed in the United States of America

INTRODUCTION

This is a story about love. Not some silly romance but true love. When I read about each of these rescue dogs, I cried and cried. And, I had a refresher course on love. Each one of these dogs is a source of inspiration for all of us.

These rescue dogs show what love is and what it is not, just by their stories alone. Each of these brave canines came from dire and painful circumstances. They were rescued by loving humans and miraculously came into the never-ending supply of God's love, expressed through their new families.

Their new humans gave as good as they could and truly experienced a renewed appreciation for unconditional love…coming expressly through one of God's greatest creatures…**The Dog**.

> *"The face of a Golden Retriever feels like home."*
> DAVID ROSENFELT

This beautiful Golden Retriever had a tough life suffering through hunger and abandonment. Underneath her shy and tentative behavior was a wellspring of love. Her rescuer patiently waited for her to settle into the home, and through it all, Sugar has had the sweetest disposition. She seems ever grateful as she teaches her lifelong loving family about love, and they in turn have helped her to gain more courage.

"I want to trust you.
My nature is to love."
SUGAR

"The better I get to know men, the more I find myself loving dogs."
CHARLES DE GAULLE

7 yrs. old
Golden Retriever

meet {sugar}

meet {**blue**}

2 yrs. old
Miniature
Schnauzer M

> *"The dog is the most faithful of animals and would be much esteemed were it not so common. Our Lord God has made His greatest gifts the commonest."*
> MARTIN LUTHER

Soulful little Blue got lucky. The forever family that adopted Blue also adopted Kenya. Originally, Kenya was supposed to help Murray, the family's ailing dog. When Murray sadly passed over to the Rainbow Bridge, Kenya needed a companion and in came Blue.

Kenya and Blue are good for each other, as Blue is nervous and Kenya is calm. Both dogs are helping their new family heal from the loss of Murray.

"I was a two-for-one special!"
BLUE

"Dogs' lives are too short. Their only fault, really."
AGNES SLIGH TURNBULL

> *"If a dog will not come to you after having looked you in the face, you should go home and examine your conscience."*
> WOODROW WILSON

Kenya came into her rescue family's home at the death of their beloved dog Murray. "Even though we thought she would help in Murray's recovery, she helped us recover from the loss of Murray."

It was the intention of the rescue family to have two dogs, so they also adopted Blue. Kenya is so well behaved and calm, and Blue is a nervous dog. "These two dogs have changed our lives!" Now, Kenya and Blue's rescuers continue to save dogs—the highly adoptable as well as "the more difficult to place" elder dogs and dogs with medical conditions.

This loving rescue family derives great satisfaction from saving dogs from high kill shelters, making home visits, and also teaching their young daughter about the value of volunteering and community service.

"Kenya and Blue now feel safe, and have a warm bed to sleep on, a human sister, and security. We love them both like crazy dog people do!"

"I'm here to spread the love!"
KENYA

meet {kenya}

2 yrs. old
Poodle/
Terrier mix

nickname:
polar bear

meet {jasper}

6 yrs. old
Blue Tick
Coonhound Mix

asper's forever family was searching for a rescue dog when they found him. His original name was Andrew. He looked like a family dog growing up and even had the name of their recently deceased father, who was a huge animal lover.

When they learned that "Andrew" had already been adopted, they were heartbroken. A few days later, the couple visited the shelter again, and there was Andrew! He had been returned for his timidity. He was panting and he was put up for adoption again. But this time was the right time.

We were afraid we could not bring about any change in Jasper, but my husband felt this was a sign from my grandfather Andrew, so we took Andrew home with us.

We changed his name to Jasper, and after some time, he slowly began to open up. The amily Golden Retriever helped him to be more confident and comfortable with people.

Jasper is now a happy and cuddley dog who loves attention, especially from people. His forever family are happy too.

"Fate decided my happy turn of events."
JASPER

———— ❦ ————

"She seemed to know from the minute she walked in the house that this was home." Roo was rescued from an animal shelter when her human was volunteering. The bond was immediate, and although bringing her home was not planned, Roo found her forever family.

Her new home had another dog, Patches, who was not well at the time. Roo respected Patches' space and seemed to energize Patches.

When Patches passed on, Roo went around the house trying to comfort the whole family.

"Not long after, I became very depressed and started to close myself off from so much." Roo, not being an especially cuddly dog who rarely slept on the bed, went into her human's bedroom, jumped onto the bed, and rested her head on her chest until calmness was restored. "She stayed with me all night."

At this point, Roo's rescuer realized that finding her was fate, and she would do anything she could to give back everything this perky dog gave that emotionally painful night. Now it's ten years later, and Roo is still enjoying movie nights and lots of fun with her new forever family.

———— ❦ ————

"I want to go wherever you go, always!"
ROO

meet {roo}

10 yrs. old
Australian
Cattle Dog

meet {crouton}

? yrs. old
Breed Unknown

> *"A man may smile and bid you hail, yet wish you to the devil;*
> *But when a good dog wags his tail, you know he's on the level."*
>
> AUTHOR UNKNOWN

———— ⚶ ————

"Give me the dog no one wants," said the kind rescuer of this sweet pup. Crouton was on death's door when she was rescued from her life of hell. Twenty-four hours from the gas chamber, she found herself resting her head on this stranger's shoulder. Although she was smelly, with matted fur and infected eyes and ears, she was saved from her nightmare by someone who cared.

"She is so beautiful and perfect, and has bonded with my two other dogs, and she adores me. Every day she thanks me with her crooked smile."

———— ⚶ ————

"I survived!"
CROUTON

———— ⚶ ————

"Dogs have given us their absolute all. We are the center of their universe. We are the focus of their love and faith and trust. They serve us in return for scraps. It is without a doubt the best deal man has ever made."
ROGER CARAS

> *"I think dogs are the most amazing creatures; they give unconditional love. For me they are the role model for being alive."*
> DAVID ROSENFELT

This elegant Papillion is now living the good life. Her rescuer was not really looking for a dog but browsing. Consequently, Penny could not be forgotten. Soon Penny was a member of the family with three cats.

Penny loves cats.

"The house feels so empty without a dog." Long walks and constant companionship fill Penny's life now. She was a puppy mill dog, and then she found her way into a Kentucky shelter.

Not anymore. Penny is living the dream.

"Penny is a little nervous on walks sometimes, but I make a point to walk where we will run into a squirrel or two, and then all is forgotten if there is a squirrel."

"I'm with my homies."
PENNY

"A dog is like a person—he needs a job and a family to be what he's meant to be."
ANDREW VACHSS

3 yrs. old
Papillion

meet {**penny**}

meet {**leon**}

6 yrs. old
Doberman
Pincher

> *"A hound will die for you, but never lie to you."*
> George R.R. Martin, *A Clash of Kings*

Leon's rescue family was looking for a dog who was good with children. They never thought of a Doberman. But this stressed-out family needed a canine like Leon.

Knowing how protective, smart, and loyal Leon has started to become, the family is beginning to trust him to watch over their young girls.

"Today, Leon is enjoying his role as second Nanny. I even caught him playing Princess tonight with Raquel as she dressed herself in a tiara, and he chose to lie down beside her."

"I've been owned by the clock. The forty-hour-plus workweek and rat race to get kids fed when they are over tired at the end of the day has left me breathless, sick, stressed, and unhappy."

"So to some, you might think I am going through a midlife crisis, but when I look at all that I've claimed back for myself over the past three days, I would actually say the crisis is over."

"I actually TRUST (Leon) to watch over the girls rather than hurt them."

"I can be trusted; I won't let you down!"
Leon

Kuwa came to her rescue family while they were looking for a puppy. A breeder said she was unwanted due to issues of time and temperament. A second Rhodesian Ridgeback arrived after the family lost two beloved dogs in the span of six months. Kito (meaning gem in Swahili) completed the family.

"We also had our son in December and couldn't ask for better dogs for him to grow up with". The family also lost a niece to murder, and during this painful time, Kito's endless happiness and immediate bond to Kuwa shined a bright light of healing in a sea of sad emotions.

Kuwa and Kito have an amazing friendship. Both are happy in their forever homes, where all the love and safety they will ever need will be generously provided.

meet {*kito*}

1 yr. old
Rhodesian
Ridgeback

meet {*kuwa*}

4 yrs. old
Rhodesian
Ridgeback

meet {casper}

2 yrs. old
Keeshond

Casper came from a puppy mill in bad condition. His rescue family had Keeshonds in the past and decided to sponsor Casper.

He has changed lives with his happiness and joy. Always happy to see his rescue family and wanting to play… he erases a bad day with his big fluffy tail.

Casper's life is now golden. He has a comfortable and safe place to grow, where he continues to be loved and cared for. He was so sad and scared when he came to his forever family. But now, he is a different dog.

"He has changed me to be a more friendly and caring person, one who reaches out to those who need a little help and is there for them"

*"I'm right here, right now,
ready for you to love me!"*

CASPER

> *"When was the last time someone was so overjoyed to see you, so brimming with love and affection that they literally ran to greet you? A dog will do that for you—ten, twenty, thirty times a day."*
>
> LIONEL FISHER

———

Mason's rescue family had previously owned rescue dogs. Upon graduation from school, one of Mason's new family members adopted him. But, his energy levels were so high there was some doubt about keeping up with him.

The plan was made to register Mason for obedience class and subsequently for a variety of other canine classes. "I saw a huge change in Mason immediately. He had an incredible drive to learn and was happiest when working."

Moving forward, this high energy canine landed spots on television, a music video, and a feature film! If that's not enough, eventually Mason became part of a performance team called, "Darn Good Dogs." He would perform for festivals and fairs all over Southern Ontario.

Mason has remained with his human family through a marriage and two babies. He has helped his owner fight depression, lack of self-confidence, and mirrored how to cultivate the joy of trying new things.

"I often wonder what would have happened to him had my mom not been successful in adopting him back in 2009; however, I also wonder what would have happened to me. Would I be as happy as I am now?

Absolutely not. I love him more than he will know. He is truly an incredible canine and my best friend."

———

"Who would have thought I'd end up in show biz?"
MASON

meet {**mason**}

6 yrs. old
Rhodesian Ridgeback/
German Shepherd Mix

meet {*daisy*}

6 yrs. old
American
Cocker Spaniel

> *"To his dog, every man is Napoleon;*
> *hence the constant popularity of dogs."*
> ALDOUS HUXLEY

Just look at that face! Daisy's winsome little smile and spatula paws must have been what won over her forever family. At six years old, the hard-to-resist Daisy came to her owners after losing her original human caretaker and a sister dog. Daisy also underwent eye surgery.

She adopted her new rescue family unconditionally. She enjoys walking the trails every day, and joy reigns supreme in her new family as she continues to spread the love.

"I'm one in a million!"
DAISY

> *"It seems to me that the good Lord in His infinite wisdom gave us three things to make life bearable—hope, jokes, and dogs. But the greatest of these was dogs."*
>
> ROBYN DAVIDSON
> *Tracks: A Woman's Solo Trek Across 1700 Miles of Australian Outback*

Dear little Otis had a rough start. He has had six or seven owners in his short lifetime, probably due to his bad manners. Jumping up onto people and licking faces. Not the most evil of deeds.

This last adoption is the last, though. Otis can feel it.

"I can't give up on him. I'm learning patience is a virtue. His face is super expressive and sad. How can you not like him?"

I'd like to think I'm changing his life more than he is mine. He is absolutely a work in progress.

"Please don't give up on me."
OTIS

1.5 yrs. old
Boxer

meet {OTIS}

12.5 yrs. old
Border Collie/
Chesapeake Bay Retriever

meet {*fiona*}

Expectantly expressive describes the visage of this dear dog. Fiona was found on the street, so little of her past is known. Most likely she was abused, as tall men and brooms or rakes send her into a tailspin.

Fiona's rescue family has changed her life by showing her kindness, love, and security by providing a safe home. Lots of meat treats also help!

Her forever family says that Fiona has changed their lives in teaching them the unlimited supply she has of unconditional love. They go for long walks together, and when their son was young, she was a constant companion. Much joy was experienced by all as the Border Collie/Chesapeake Bay Retriever mix tried to herd the family children as they ran around!

"I love my life!"

FIONA

> *"A well-trained dog will make no attempt to share your lunch. He will just make you feel so guilty that you cannot enjoy it."*
>
> HELEN THOMAS

Vedder and Zoe's rescue human wanted to adopt a dog or two that really needed a home. Vedder was on death row when he was rescued by his forever human who was suffering from depression and anxiety. "Giving him love and having him by my side provided such comfort and healing to me. Whenever I am down, he really seems to know and always sits by my side. I love him immensely."

Vedder's life has also changed in a big way. He is cherished by his human family and receives all that he needs to thrive. They even decided to get him a companion. Enter stage left is Zoe. She was a street puppy and so thin. "I can't imagine how she survived!"

"Being such a tiny dog, we thought she would be a sweet, gentle pup, but she turned out to be quite spunky and feisty. Vedder was intimidated at first by her wackiness, but they soon became good buddies, of course."

"Good job we are both so adorable; we really got lucky."

VEDDER & ZOE

meet {zoe}

2.5 yrs. old
Toy Rat Terrier

6 yrs. old
Jack Russell/
Rat Terrier Mix

meet {vedder}

meet {*millie*}

1 yr. old
English
Cocker Spaniel

> *"The only creatures that are evolved enough to convey pure love are dogs and infants."*
> JOHNNY DEPP

Sweet little Millie made it to the top! She started out life with a family who really couldn't care for her, and she resided in a cage in the basement for up to sixteen hours a day.

Luckily for Millie, her rescue family agreed to take her in and give her a different kind of life.

Now, little Millie has a forever family and a sister dog named Sadie. When Sadie slipped a disk and was paralyzed, Millie would not leave her side until she recovered.

Today, Millie and Sadie run and run together, since their humans moved to the country. They have a marvelous life full of adventure, fresh air, toys, and love. Especially the love.

"I went from rags to riches!"
MILLIE

"A dog reflects the family life. Whoever saw a frisky dog in a gloomy family, or a sad dog in a happy one? Snarling people have snarling dogs, dangerous people have dangerous ones."
ARTHUR CONAN DOYLE
—The Case-Book of Sherlock Holmes

> *"Dogs are wise. They crawl away in a quiet corner and lick their wounds and do not rejoin the world until they are whole once more."*
>
> AGATHA CHRISTIE

River's story is quite heartbreaking but has a happy ending. Curled up in a ball at the end of the shelter cages was River. She had many behavioral problems and severe anxiety. She had been adopted and returned twice, and had spent most of her entire life in a cage.

Luckily for River, her rescue human had a lot of experience with dogs, growing up with them, working at animal hospitals, volunteering, and as a groomer.

The woman at the animal shelter was taken aback when River was chosen for a family. She truly was an abused and frightened dog.

With the wisdom of her rescue family who knew what to do and not do, River is a different dog. She has a new canine friend called Chief and a forever family.

"All she needed was to know that she was staying and that we weren't giving up on her. The more she realized this, the more healed she became. She is so unbelievably affectionate and sweet and gentle."

River was exactly what the whole family needed after losing two family dogs in succession. "She is exactly what we all needed, and I am so incredibly grateful that she is in our lives. Every morning she wakes me up by coming into my room and wagging her tail so hard on the wall because she's just SO happy to be here and to see that I'm awake. I literally can't imagine my life without her."

"You believed in me and I'm staying."

RIVER

1.5 yrs. old
Golden Retriever

meet {river}

6 yrs. old
German Shepherd/
Rottweiler/Leonberger

meet {**maya**}

> *"Qui me amat, amet et canem meum.*
> *(Who loves me will love my dog also.)"*
> BERNARD OF CLAIRVAUX

The shelters were full of dogs after hurricane Katrina. "We decided to choose a rescue (dog)." Although Maya has been dealt a myriad of health problems, she was nevertheless adopted by a humane forever family.

"Maya has changed my life in so many ways!" Her canine rescuer is a very shy person. So, as the bond between dog and human strengthened, they helped each other to grow and gain confidence.

"I started taking Maya to training classes. With Maya, I am very confident and feel I can do anything."

When her human became ill and had to go to the hospital, Maya would come to visit and cheer up the entire ward.

Her kind new human family deals with Maya's hip displaysia, and her rare kind of IBS, which requires that her meals be prepared with home-cooked Kangaroo! She also has thyroid problems and needed knee surgery.

When asked if they would adopt her again, the response is, "I would do it in a heartbeat; her love is unconditional! She's the best dog you could ever meet!"

"I survived Hurricane Katrina!"
MAYA

Lovely Lucy was found at seven months wandering on some walking trails. She was quite skinny and remained at the Humane Society for a considerable amount of time. Her rescue humans said, "It was a long haul of obedience classes and persistent training to get her to the point she is today." Lucy was very food insecure and lacked the puppy-like behaviors typical of her age. "She now is silly and lovable and a joy to call our dog."

"I don't worry about food now; there's plenty."
Lucy

Handsome Linus was rescued at the age of seven months by the same rescue family as Lucy. His previous family did not have time for him, and it showed with his untrained behaviors. His new family has taken the time and effort to have him properly trained. Linus is a lovable little guy with unending energy and the desire to play. He is very tactile and loves to be touched. He loves Lucy! "Although Lucy grumbles when Linus wants to cuddle or play, we know that she secretly adores him!"

"Someone has time for me now."
Linus

meet {*lucy*}

3 yrs. old
Border Collie

meet {*linus*}

1 yr. old
Maltese

meet {xena}

9 months old
Boston Terrier

Rescued from a puppy mill, nine-month-old Xena had a lucky break.
This priceless pup was born blind and would not have had a very
good life if not for her forever rescue family.

Xena is a smart and feisty little female who does not let her disability
get in her way of having fun at all! She loves everyone and continues
to surprise humans with the fact that she is blind.

"I don't need eyesight to see who you really are."
XENA

> *"Not Carnegie, Vanderbilt, and Astor together could have raised money enough to buy a quarter share in my little dog."*
> ERNEST THOMPSON SETON

———————

Tiny Tyson surely demonstrates the adage of, "The eyes are the windows to the soul." His forever human rescued this badly abused tyke who was extremely anxious and nervous due to his past history.

Tyson has changed his rescuers' lives by bringing joy into the home. "I realized that a house without pets just doesn't feel like a home."

As Tyson came to realize that he would consistently be treated with love and gentle respect, he in turn modeled those behaviors.

"Tyson is now a happy, healthy little love bug. His greatest comforts are a cozy blanket, a crinkle toy, and a soft lap to snuggle into."

As his painful memories fade, Tyson continues to trust and bloom with the universal salve of love.

———————

"I'm tougher than I look!"
TYSON

meet {tyson}

5 yrs. old
Chihuahua

1 yr. old

Golden Lab/
Siberian
Husky Mix

6.5 yrs. old

German Shephe
Lab Mix

meet {maggie}   meet {chloe}

> *"Acquiring a dog may be the only opportunity*
> *a human ever has to choose a relative."*
> MORDECAI SIEGALL

This pair of pups came together in a circuitous way. Their forever household started out with a dog named Khalua that became very anxious and distressed when the family left the home—destroying everything in his path. Trying to find the best solution to this increasingly annoying problem, the family decided to adopt another dog to keep Khalua company. That dog was the beautiful Chloe. Six years apart, Chloe kept Khalua young, and with that, all the behavior problems were solved.

Eventually, Khalua developed severe seizures and needed to be put to sleep. Chloe was most unhappy without her pal. Soon Chloe stopped eating, drinking, and playing. She lost weight. Chloe was severely depressed.

This is when her forever family decided to start looking for another companion for Chloe. The family decided to bring Chloe with them to pick out her new friend. A litter of puppies had been abandoned, and so the family had a private meeting with two of the pups. "That's when we noticed Chloe actually playing with 'Mustard', later named Maggie. We knew they were the perfect match!"

"They now have become inseparable, and we can honestly say Maggie rescued Chloe!" Chloe started to eat and play again as if she had a newfound zest for living.

"We are best pals and never lonely anymore."
MAGGIE & CHLOE

Gioia (pronounced "Joy-a") was a shell of a dog when she came to live with her rescue family. A puppy mill survivor, this dear little female had been used for breeding since birth. "Mills are terrible places, hell on earth for dogs. When a dog is no longer able to breed pups for profit, they are often disposed of." This poor little mite needed a loving family and she found one.

Lupo was another dog at the same foster home as Gioia. Fortunately for Lupo, the decision was made to adopt both Gioia and Lupo. Timid Lupo became best buddies with Gioia, and the two never looked back. Gioia allowed Lupo into her sacred crate, and the two would sleep completely entangled. This was their healing.

"I'm a happy little guy now."
LUPO

"I have come alive!"
GIOIA

meet {LUPO}

2 yrs. old
Chihuahua/
Rat Terrier

9 yrs. old
Chihuahua/
Dachshund

meet {Gioia}

meet {jaks}

5 yrs. old
Chocolate Lab/
Redbone Coonhound

"Beautiful, chocolatey Jaks with the sparkling coat was on a kill list. But not for long. Jaks' rescuers had recently lost a puppy in a tragic accident and were looking for a mature dog. "We were looking for a dog that would be able to walk into our lives and fill the void."

Jaks was able to help his new family with the grieving process of losing two dogs in two years. "He walked right into our home and became one of us. He had never walked up stairs, or most likely ever played with toys before us, but he instantly felt our love."

Jaks' incredibly shiny and healthy coat is due to a raw food diet that was recommended for his Lyme disease. Also surviving a car accident and being shot with a pellet, he had already been through a lot in his short life. But now, Jaks' forever family provides warmth, nutritious food, plenty of rest, and, of course, an abundance of love.

"I never knew I was a Royal dog until I met my new family."

JAKS

> *"It came to me that every time I lose a dog they take a piece of my heart with them. And every new dog that comes into my life gifts me with a piece of their heart. If I live long enough, all the components of my heart will be dog, and I will become as generous and loving as they are."*
>
> AUTHOR UNKNOWN

After losing their sixteen-year-old rescue dog, Phineas's potential family had a huge hole in their hearts. Then they spotted this four-month-old pup with the gigantic paws at the shelter. He won their hearts over completely, and the family brought him home immediately.

Settling in, Phineas was a wild and crazy puppy that had to undergo surgery to remove chewed pieces of plastic and string... all costing the family quite a bundle. After the surgery the vet warned the family that this was who Phineas was, and they had to make a decision. The bottom line was they loved him. Therefore, with no hesitation this loving family made the decision to keep Phineas regardless of the financial outlay and make him part of their permanent family.

Thus, once again, the power of love over money and all other obstacles won out, and the dog who gives so much wins!

"I give the best kisses."

PHINEAS

1 yr. old
Shepherd Cross

meet {phineas}

PHINEAS

meet {liily}

6 yrs. old
Samoyed

> *"Puppies are nature's remedy for feeling unloved;*
> *plus numerous other ailments of life."*
> RICHARD ALLEN PALM

Liily came from a high kill shelter and went on to help the heartbroken human who lost a canine companion of sixteen years. She helped her new human deal with loss, and they both bonded to each other out of need. And they needed each other equally. "Liily is truly a godsend, and I swear she is an old companion from a past life. I can't imagine my life without her, and we thank our stars every day that our paths crossed and we were able to rescue each other."

A few months after adopting Liily, her human mom met the human love of her life. Liily and her new family are inseparable! "Now we have a complete and happy little family."

"I found my human companion."
LIILY

> *"Some men can be good 'horse whisperers,'*
> *and many dogs can be wonderful 'man whisperers.'"*
> ERIK PEVERNAGIE

Diminutive Toash was a street dog brought to a kill shelter, then sent to a foster home for temporary shelter. "It took three days for it to be clear that he would never be leaving, and in a couple of weeks we adopted him into our family to stay forever."

Toash's new human female had been experiencing sadness and difficulties for a few years. Opening her home to foster and rescue dogs helped heal her heart and bring natural happiness back into her life.

"Coming home to his little face every day, knowing how much he depends on us and how much he loves us, is just like therapy and adds so much joy to my life."

Now, Toash has a warm bed, healthy food, and an abundance of love. All of these ministrations helped heal his skin condition, let alone his own broken heart.

> *"I'm never planning on running away from home."*
> TOASH

meet {*toash*}

4 yrs. old
Chihuahua

meet {joey}

7 yrs. old
Shih Tzu

Dogs don't rationalize. They don't hold anything against a person.
They don't see the outside of a human but the inside of a human."
CESAR MILLAN *(dog trainer)*

Serendipity played a part in adorable Joey's adoption. His rescue human happened to be watching a television program announcing his ready-to-adopt status. "My husband and I had never talked about getting a dog, but this felt like the time."

Unfortunately, hard-to-resist Joey had attracted others who were interested in adopting him too. "I was sad to hear that I was eighth in line and needed to go through an interview process, and my heart crashed with sadness."

Two weeks later, Joey became a bonafide family member. This dear little Shih Tzu was put up for adoption due to the death of one of his previous humans and not being able to go into the retirement facility of the other. "To this day, we always say how terribly sad and heartbreaking it would be to give Joey away. It would never happen."

Now sweet Joey has his new family. "We are a family of one child. We tried dearly to have our daughter and always wished that I would have another, possibly a son. Joey is my furry son; I love him just the same."

"I've started a new life. I was so sad but now I'm not."

———

Handsome Duke came to his rescue human from St. Maarten's, where he had been in a sanctuary. When the sanctuary closed, all the dogs had to be moved to Canada. Sadly, Duke was the last of ten dogs to be adopted and thus remained in foster care. That is until his rescuer saw him and had to have him.

Duke's foster mother and rescue mother worked hard to make the transition to his forever home easy for him. Duke had high anxiety and was very nervous. "In the beginning it was tough, as he really was scared of EVERYTHING. It took me a day and a half to get him to eat. He is really coming around. It has been two months, and he is becoming playful. He is excited to eat; and he's starting to play with my Boston."

Duke has helped his rescue mom heal from two significant relationships. The loss of a human relationship and that of her beloved dog Mabel. "It has been beyond devastating…a pain I can't describe. Duke has helped me heal a lot just by seeing him become more happy, comfortable, loving, and playful".

"He has definitely helped heal my heart just a bit more every day."

———

"I had to come a long way to find my happiness."
DUKE

meet {duke}

4 yrs. old
Black Mouth Cur

3 yrs. old
Beagle/Boxer

meet {roscoe}

> *"Those who teach the most about humanity aren't always human."*
> DONALD L. HICKS, *Look into the Stillness*

As soon as Roscoe's future forever family saw his picture on a Pet finders site, his fate did a 360. Sweet Roscoe was on a kill list but was miraculously rescued and in his new home about a week later thanks to the Internet and his kind human family.

"As soon as I saw his picture, I thought he was the dog for us, and when I met him I knew. Roscoe is friendly and happy, and his big brown eyes melted my heart."

Roscoe's new family feels their life has changed for the better. "He brings out the best in us, and he makes me smile after a hard day with a wag of his tail and a kiss."

Roscoe is always happy and brings positive energy into his new home. He goes on play-dates with other dogs and is spoiled with love and devotion. "Roscoe is awesome." I'd call this a win-win.

"I've finally got a life! Complete with play-dates!"
ROSCOE

All the paw prints in this book are the actual
paw prints from the rescue dogs.